Foxes

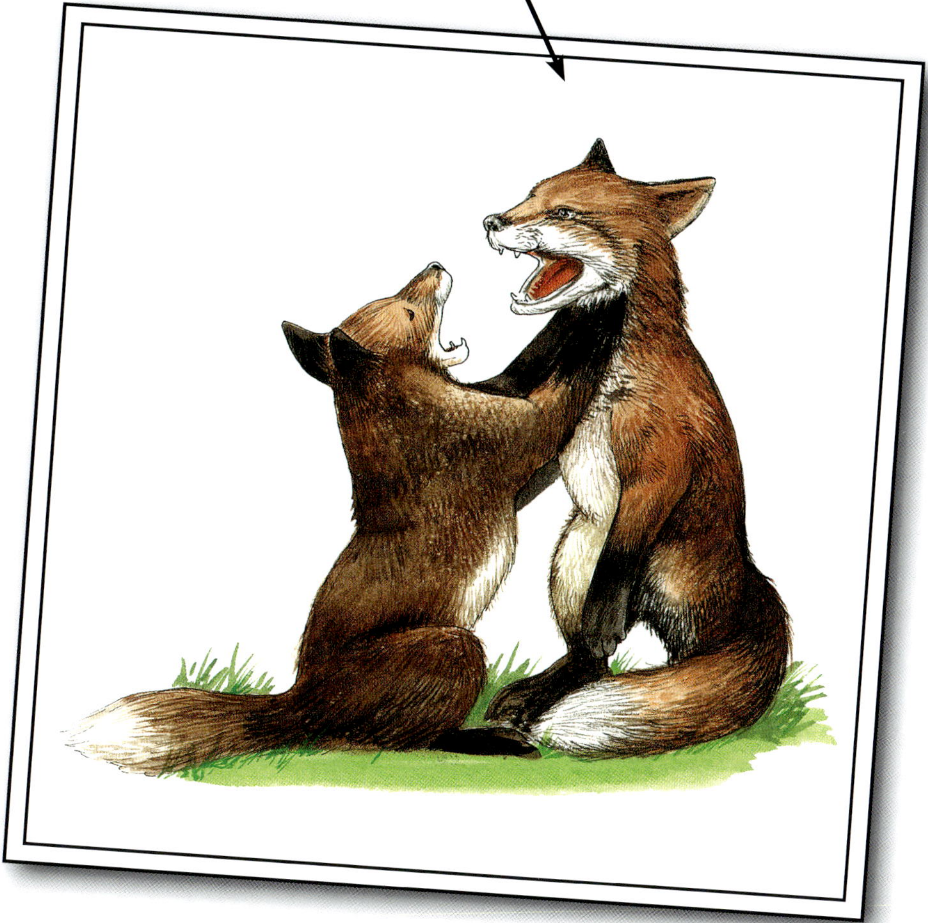

This is a dog fox.

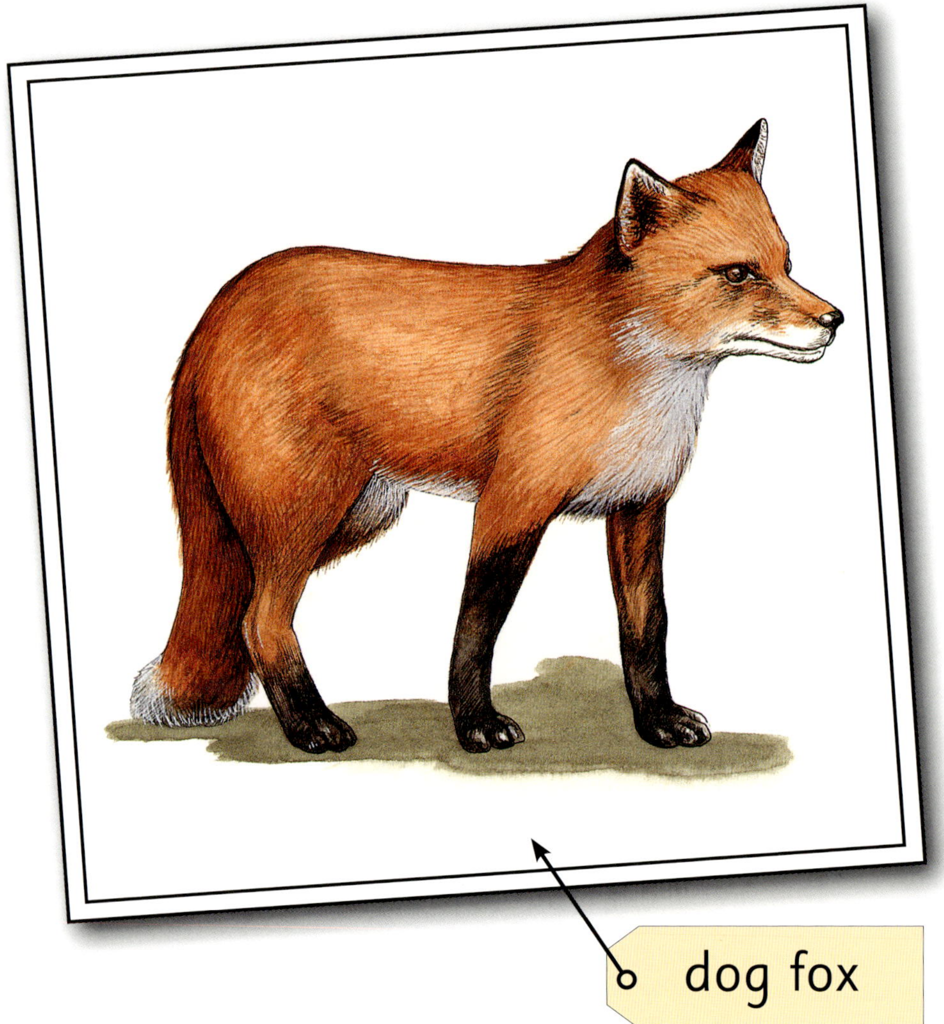

This is a vixen.

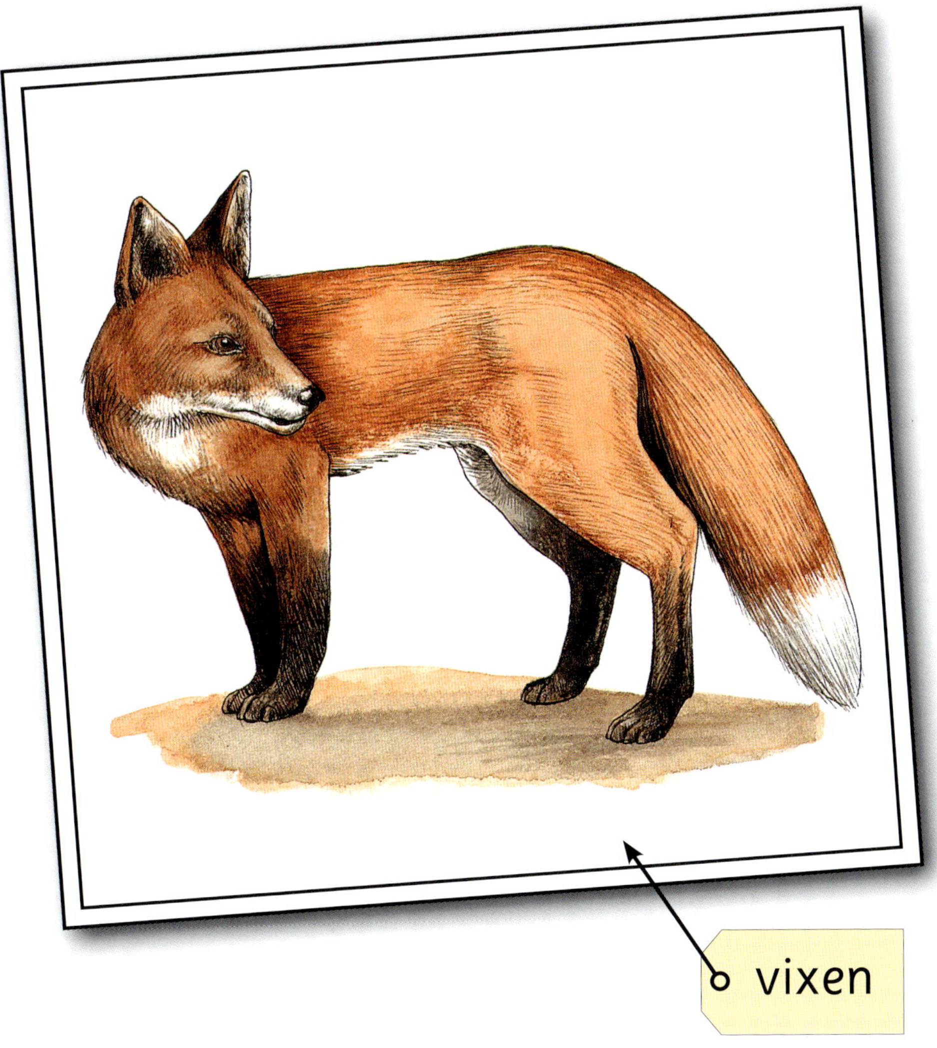

This vixen has three cubs.

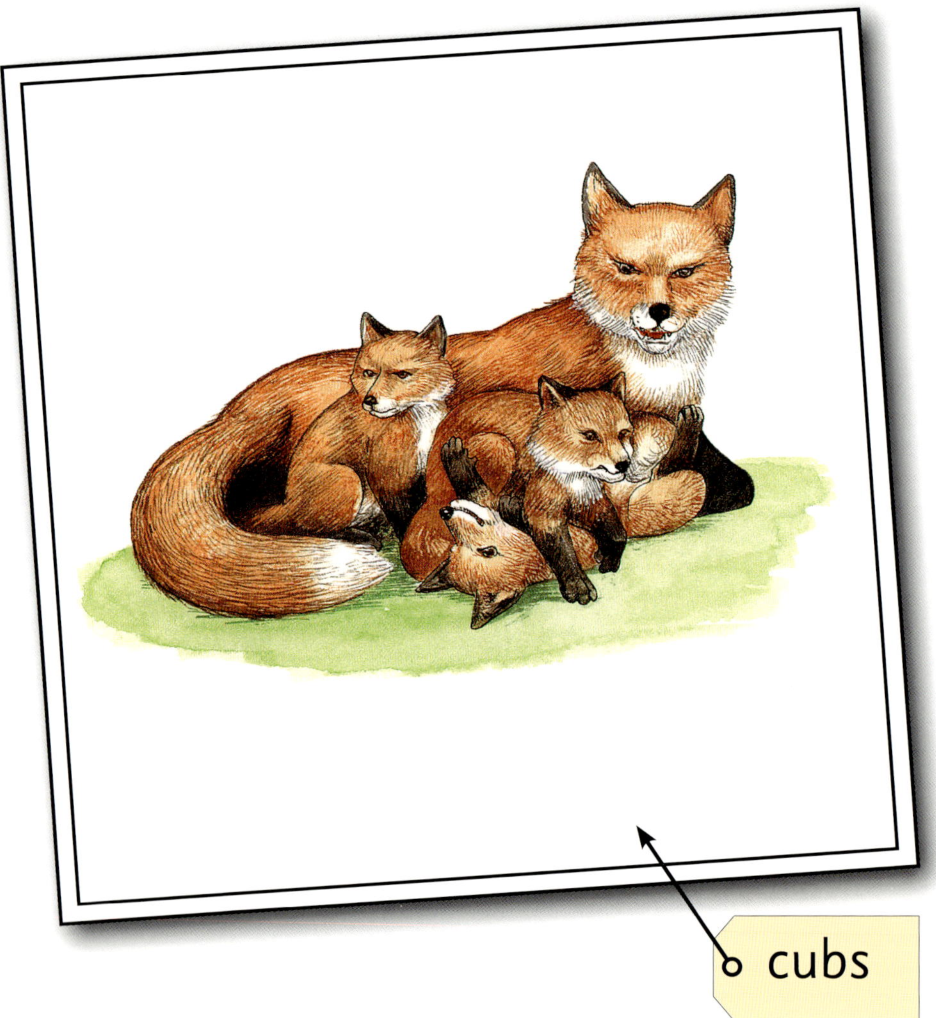

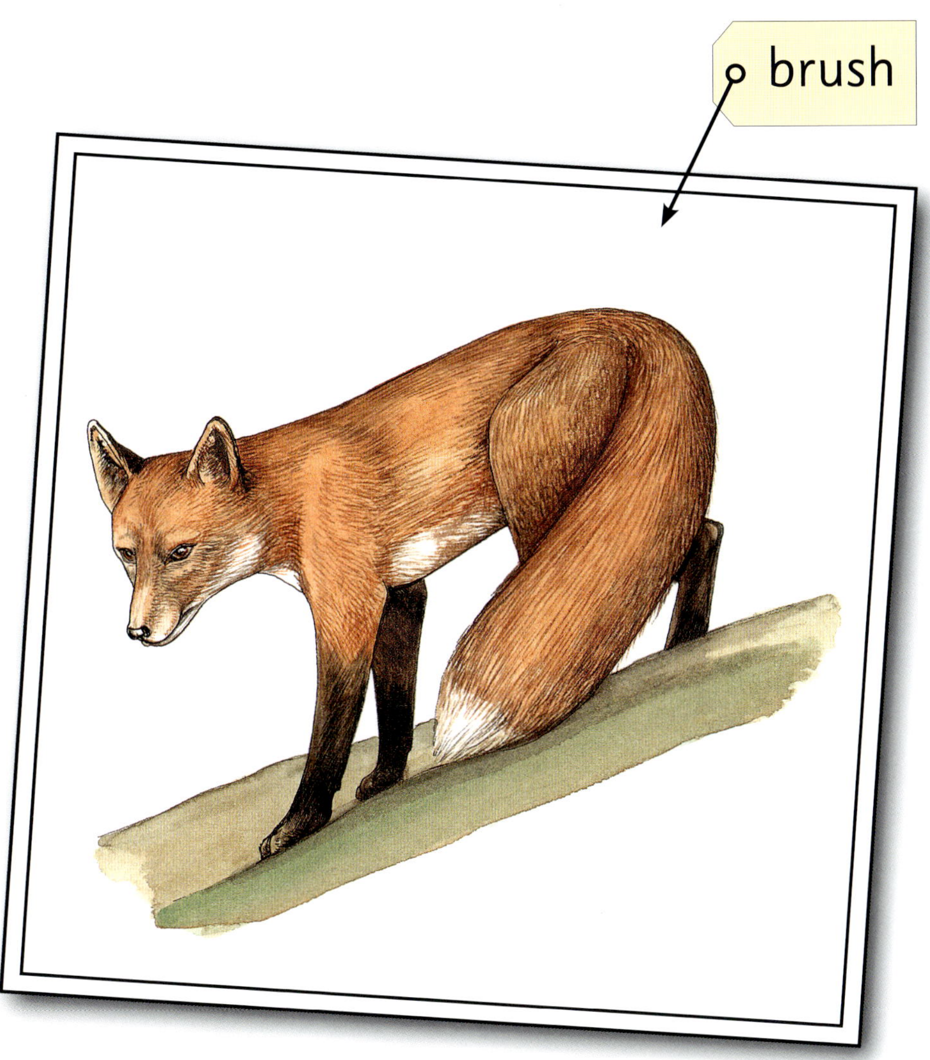

A fox's tail is a brush.

Foxes live in dens.

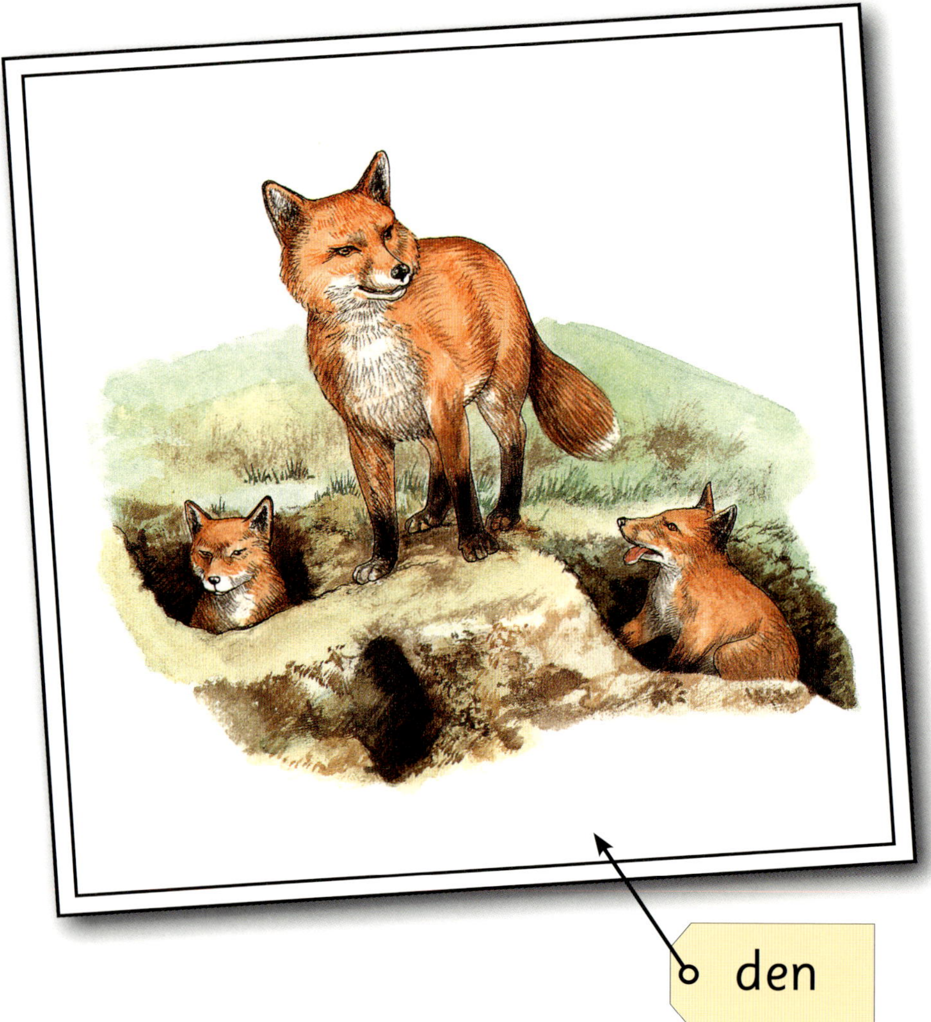

Foxes dig dens under the ground.

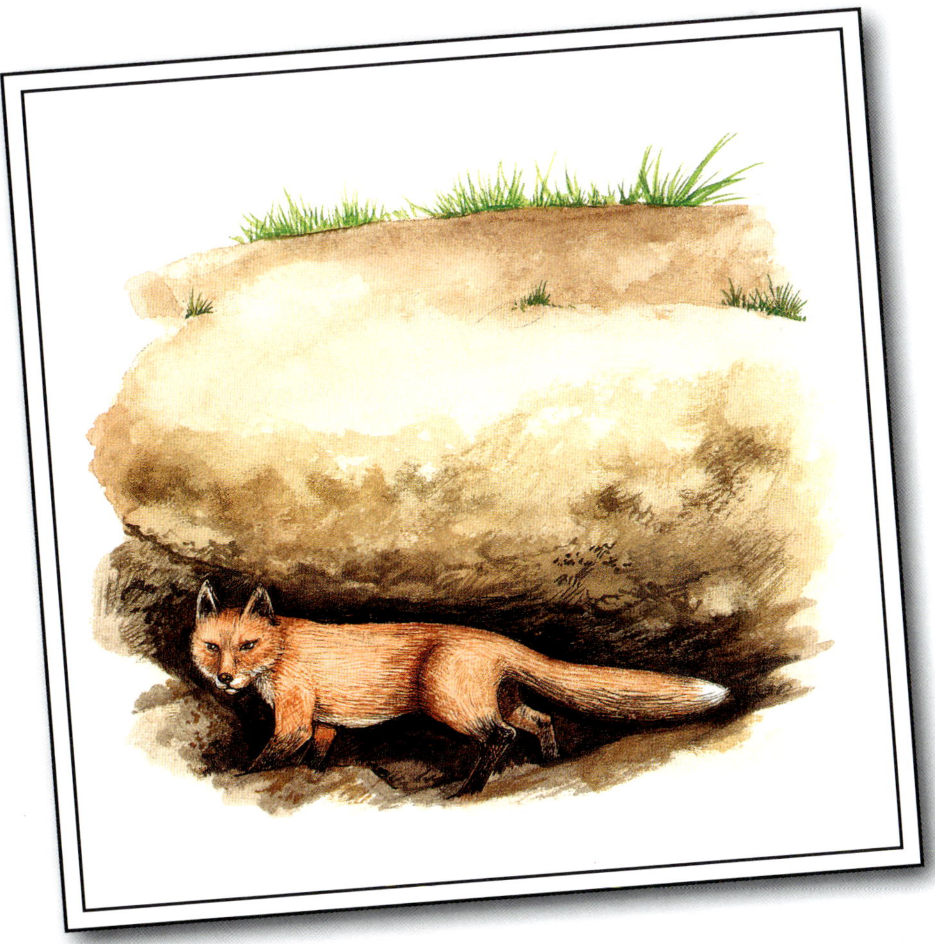

Foxes hunt in the dark.

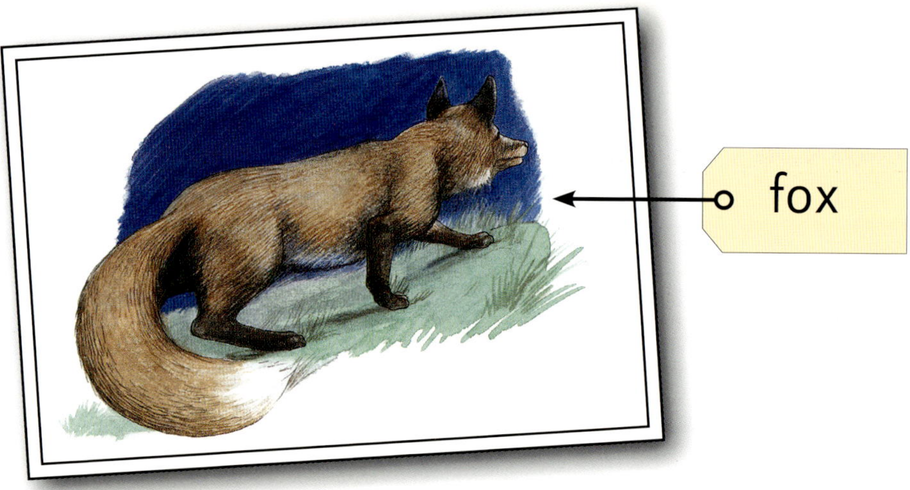

Look out, rabbit!

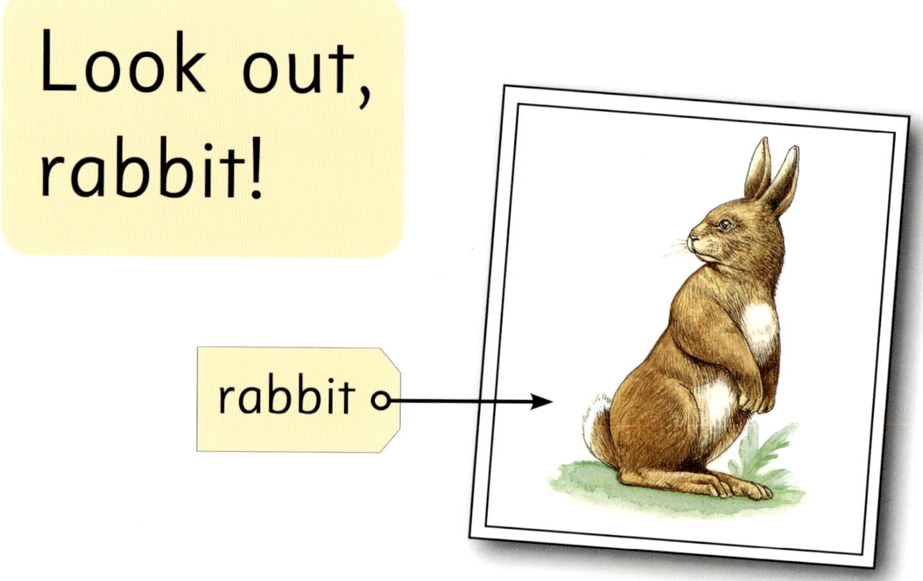